W9-DIV-627

Kore Yamazaki

Frau Faust

1

contents

Frau Faust

Chapter 1:
The Man From the Fairy Tale
3

Chapter 2:
Waiting in the Forest
47

Chapter 3:
That Belongs to Me
85

The Invisible Museum
125

A LONG TIME AGO, IN A FAR-OFF PLACE, THERE WAS A MAN NAMED FAUST.
FAUST WAS A VERY, VERY GREEDY MAN.
ONE DAY, FAUST CAME ACROSS A DEMON, WHO SPOKE TO HIM THUS:
CH. 1
"IF THOU GIVEST ME THY SOUL...
...I SHALL DO THINE EVERY BIDDING UNTIL THE PREORDAINED MOMENT OF THY DEATH."
TEMPTED BY THIS OFFER, FAUST SIGNED A CONTRACT WITH THE DEMON.
KTNK
KTNK
...AND THEN HE DID EVERY SINGLE THING THAT HE'D EVER DESIRED.
RATTLE
RATTLE
RATTLE
WHAT HAPPENED TO FAUST AFTER THAT?
HM?
AFTER HE FULFILLED ALL HIS DESIRES...
...CAME THE DAY OF HIS DEATH.
ON THAT DAY, THE DEMON BROKE HIS NECK AND KILLED HIM.

Chapter 1:
The Man From the Fairy Tale

DID YOU HEAR THERE WERE INQUISITORS AROUND HERE?
NO KIDDING? ARE THERE DEMONS OR WITCHES ABOUT?
IT SMELLS.
POSI-TIVELY REEKS.
A FAMILIAR KIND OF SMELL.

HASN'T CHANGED A BIT.
SST
TSST
FSHH
TCH!
THIS MUST BE IT. NOW I NEED A MARK.
ZZAT

TO THINK YOU WOULD HAVE US INQUISITORS HELP YOU MOVE THAT THING...
GREAK
STILL WANING.
I'D BE TAKING ON UNNECESSARY RISK IF I DON'T WAIT FOR THE NEW MOON.
ME TOO.
I'VE GOT SO MUCH PAPER-WORK TO DO.
AT LEAST IT'S OVER WITH NOW. LET'S GO BACK TO THE BARRACKS.
THE CONSTANT TRAVEL IS SO ANNOYING, THOUGH.
HEY, THEY WERE SHORT ON HELP. AND BESIDES, IT'S TOP-SECRET.

...
THAT SMELL. IT'S THE SAME.
IT'S SO ACTIVE NOW. NOT LIKE THE PAST. WEREN'T SO MANY PEOPLE BACK THEN.
HEY! CATCH THAT BOY!
HE'S A BOOK THIEF!
WHOA!
THUD

ON YOUR FEET, THIEF! YOU'LL SPEND THE NIGHT IN A CELL!
THANKS, MA'AM.
HM? YOU MEAN HIM?
WHY...?
I'D SAY YOU OWE ME ONE NOW, MARK.
JUST A LITTLE SLEIGHT OF HAND.
WHAT?! THE THIEF TURNED INTO A SCRAP OF PAPER!!
H—
HOW DID YOU ...?
H—

JOLT
THERE YOU ARE, MARION.
THMP
ZWIP
GOOD DAY, MOTHER!
H-HERE I AM, MOTHER! UM, LISTEN...
WHY, THANK Y...
KSHIF
OH, MY GOOD-NESS.
PLEASE ACCEPT THIS MEAGER TOKEN OF MY APPRE-CIATION.
I AM BUT A HUMBLE TRAVELER WHO HAPPENED UPON YOUR DELIGHTFUL SON JUST NOW.
JOHANNA, AT YOUR SERVICE.
TEP

OH, HOW LONG HAS IT BEEN SINCE I...
OH MY WORD! THIS IS THE KUCHEN FROM THE SHOP ON THE CORNER OF THIRD STREET!

WHA—?!
SO I CAN GET MORE DIRT ON YOU AND TIGHTEN THE SCREWS.
HMM? WHAT, ARE YOU KIDDING?

WHY DID YOU DEMAND TO MEET MY MOTHER?

DON'T WORRY, I WON'T TELL HER YOU'RE A THIEF.
LEAVE HER OUT OF THIS!

WELL? WHY WERE YOU STEALING BOOKS?

HEE HEE HEE!
AS LONG AS YOU DON'T TELL HER ABOUT MY "SLEIGHT OF HAND."
...

MY FATHER'S BUSINESS FAILED...AND THE DEBT COLLECTORS TOOK WHATEVER THEY THOUGHT THEY COULD SELL.
THAT INCLUDED THESE.
IT'S STILL A STRETCH TO CLAIM YOU'RE "NOT A THIEF."
I'M NOT A THIEF.
THESE WERE *MY* BOOKS TO BEGIN WITH.
A HISTORY BOOK?
BUT STILL!
THEY COULD HAVE TAKEN ANYTHING ELSE FROM ME...BUT NOT THE BOOKS.
BOOKS ARE LIKE TREASURE. WITH ENOUGH EDUCATION, EVEN A POOR MAN CAN BE RESPECTED AND FIND WORK...
CONTI-NENTAL YEAR 372.
FLIP

HUH?
WHAT HAPPENED IN 372?
WHY DID IT SPLIT OFF?
UH...
THE INDEPENDENCE OF ALBION FROM THE BYZANTIA EMPIRE?
BECAUSE BYZANZ STOPPED TRADING WITH THEM, AND THEY NEEDED RESOURCES, SO THEY...
THAT'S THE OUTWARD NARRATIVE.
IN FACT, THE DUCHY OF ALBION HAD ITS OWN ARRANGEMENT WITH THE NORTHERN ALLIANCE.
BOTH SIDES WERE ADVANCED SEAFARERS, YOU SEE. BYZANTIA PANICKED, TRIED TO TUG ON THE CHAIN, AND ALBION SLIPPED RIGHT THROUGH THE COLLAR.
AND THAT'S THE REAL STORY.
BYZANTIA WAS ALREADY WEAKENED BY THEN, IN FACT...
AND THEN?! THEN WHAT HAPPENED?!

BOOKS ARE THE FORTUNE OF OUR FOREBEARS.
BUT DON'T TAKE THEIR WORDS AT FACE VALUE. DON'T FIXATE ON THEM.
TAKE A MULTI-FACETED VIEW OF THINGS.
THAT'S HOW YOU TAKE IN NEW KNOWL-EDGE.
WOULDN'T YOU FEEL STUPID GOING TO JAIL OVER A HANDFUL OF BOOKS?
...I SUP-POSE.
I KNOW!
I'VE GOT A FEW DAYS TO KILL—I'M WILLING TO BE YOUR TEACHER FOR A BIT.
HUH?!
WHAP
WHAT SUBJECT DO YOU PREFER? LANGUAGE? HISTORY? MATH? ALCHEMY?
I THINK YOU'LL FIND THAT I KNOW QUITE A BIT.
...

AHEM!
...WHAT DO YOU WANT FROM ME?
AHA! YOU'RE LEARNING ALREADY.
I AM ON A SEARCH.
SEARCH?
FOR A STUPID MUTT OF MINE THAT WANDERED OFF.
FOR SOME REASON, IT TENDS TO SHOW UP IN A CERTAIN SPOT.
I JUST NEED YOU TO OPEN THE DOOR TO THIS PLACE ON THE NIGHT OF A NEW MOON.

YEP, JUST ONE DOOR. THAT'S ALL.
ANYWAY, THANKS FOR PUTTING ME UP!
TAK TAK TAK
HUH?!
AT MY HOUSE?! WAIT, JOHANNA!
DOOR...?
SHE'S SO STRANGE...

WHAT'S THIS?
AN APPLE.
HOW MUCH DOES IT COST? WHERE IS IT FROM?
ONE COPPER... SOURCE: ALBION.
HEE HEE HEE HEE!
MOST HUMAN BEINGS CAN'T REMEMBER A THING UNLESS THEY'RE IN A DESPERATE SITUATION.
BECAUSE YOU'RE CRAMMING IT INTO ME LIKE THERE'S NO TOMORROW, JOHANNA...
HEE HEE HEE!
THE YOUNG MIND RETAINS INFORMATION LIKE A SPONGE.

HM?
WHAT IS IT, JOHANNA?
NEVER READ IT? IT'S A VERY FAMOUS FAIRY TALE.
THE LIFE OF DR. FAUST...?
THERE WAS ONCE A SMART BUT GREEDY MAN NAMED FAUST.
HE SIGNED A CONTRACT WITH A DEMON NAMED MEPHISTO, AND THEY COMMITED ALL KINDS OF WICKED ACTS TOGETHER.
THAT BOOK IS AN ENTERTAINING ACCOUNT OF ALL OF THOSE EVIL DEEDS.
I'M FAMILIAR... BUT I DIDN'T KNOW THEY MADE IT INTO A BOO...
HEE!
FLIP
ペラッ

UM... JOHANNA?
HEE!
HEE!
HEE HEE HEE HEE HEE HEE!
WELL, SURE, THAT'S WHAT FAIRY TALES ARE LIKE.
RECALLING THE DETAILS REMINDS ME OF WHAT A MONSTER HE IS.
POISONING THE WELL, ROASTING AND EATING THE GRAVE-KEEPING DRAGON...
...IN-DEED.
A FAIRY TALE IS CONSTRUCTED FROM TRUTH, FACT, AND FANTASY ALIKE.
HM?
STUDENTS?

DID YOU GO TO SCHOOL, TOO?
HUH?
YES. THE CHURCH HERE ALSO ACTS AS A SCHOOL. AS LONG AS YOU PAY, YOU CAN ATTEND.
SEEMS TO BE A COMMON STYLE NOW.
WELL...
I DID ATTEND SCHOOL THAT WAY BEFORE.
I REALLY, TRULY ENJOYED MY TIME THERE.
BUT THEN WE COULDN'T COME UP WITH THE MONEY...I NEARLY HAD THE CREDIT FOR THE NEXT GRADE, TOO.
I HADN'T REALIZED THAT A PLACE I ONCE SO EASILY ATTENDED COULD COME TO FEEL SO IMPOSSIBLY DISTANT.

I'D GIVEN UP ON THE IDEA OF STUDYING EVER AGAIN.
THANK YOU, JOHANNA.
...YOU HAVEN'T FORGOTTEN THAT I'M BLACKMAILING YOU, HAVE YOU?
WH-WHAT?
IT'S TOO SUDDEN...
WE'LL BE PARTING ON THE MORROW.
THE NEW MOON IS TONIGHT.
HEE HEE!
URK!

YOU... NEVER ACTUALLY THREATENED ME ONCE.
HEE HEE HEE!

IT WAS JUST FOR A FEW DAYS, REMEMBER? CONSIDER YOURSELF LUCKY I WON'T BE THREATENING YOU ANYMORE.

SHE REALLY IS...
...QUITE STRANGE...

TOK
TOK
TOK
TOK

FORGOT TO BUY SOME-THING.

WHAT'S THE MATTER?
JEALOUS?
JUST KEEP WAITING THERE GRINNING...
AND NOW I'VE FOUND YOU AGAIN AT LAST.
REMEMBER, *YOU* WERE THE ONE WHO LEFT *ME* BEHIND.
...MEPHISTO.

SHLUF
FWAP!
I FINALLY FOUND THAT 200-YEAR-OLD ALCHEMY TEXT I WAS LOOKING FOR!
YOUR SECOND ALL-NIGHT-ER?
HEY!
WHY DON'T YOU TAKE A BREAK?
MMM.
CREAK
SHOULD'A PUT THAT LINE IN THE CONTRACT ABOUT GIVING ME A BODY THAT NEEDS NO SLEEP OR REST.
HUMAN BEINGS FALL TO RUIN IF THEY DO NOT REST.
YOU DIDN'T TAMPER WITH YOUR BODY, REMEM-BER.
WHAT'S THE BIG IDEA?
THWP
SIT DOWN.
TUG
YOU WERE THE ONE WHO ARGUED AGAINST THAT AT THE TIME.

YOU WANTED ME TO REST.
SO WAKE ME UP IN AN HOUR AND A HALF.
AS YOU COM-MAND...
...MASTER.
A DREAM.
IT'S SUN-DOWN ...

AND I DON'T HEAR HIS VOICE ANYMORE.
I'M JUST NOT...
...USED TO IT YET.
AWOOOO...
WITHOUT THE MOON TO LIGHT THE WAY...
...IT'S VERY DARK OUT.
FWOOOSH
YOU SURE PACKED A LOT.
J-JUST IN CASE. IT'S A BIT SCARY.

THE CHURCH?
THAT'S WHERE YOUR DOG WILL BE?
AS I SAID, HE'S VERY STUPID.
ARE YOU REALLY LEAVING, JOHANNA?
OUR BARGAIN WAS JUST FOR A FEW DAYS.

BUT ...
WITH YOUR SMARTS, YOU SHOULD BE GOOD ON YOUR OWN NOW.

RUB
RUB
FINE, FINE!
I'LL SHOW YOU SOMETHING VERY SPECIAL AND RARE.
JUST STOP MOPING.
OKAY?

CREE
LIKE THIS?

CREAK

THAT WASN'T THE PROBLEM, THOUGH...
OKAY.

...?
"COME IN."
JUST TELL ME TO COME IN.
WHA?
YES.
YOU GO INSIDE... AND THEN INVITE ME IN.
TEP
WHEN YOU'RE UNCLEAN LIKE ME, YOU NEED AN INVITATION TO GET INTO THESE SACRED PLACES.
SEE, I'M UNDER A BIT OF A CURSE.
THIS IS THE REASON I CALLED YOU HERE.
WHAT WAS THAT ABOUT?

C-C-CURSE?!
DON'T WORRY, IT'S NOT CONTAGIOUS.

I DIDN'T KNOW THIS WAS BENEATH THE CHURCH...
MOST CHURCHES BUILT DURING THE ERA OF THE THREE KINGDOMS' WAR ARE THE SAME.
VESTIGES OF FORTS.

DID YOU ALREADY KNOW ABOUT THIS?

HUH?
YES.
I WAS HERE SOME DECADES AGO.
BUT THE LEAD WAS A DUD.

KTOK
KTOK
KTOK
KTOK

THAT WASN'T A LIE.
JOHANNA, ARE YOU...?
YOU SAID YOU WERE LOOKING FOR YOUR DOG, RIGHT?
ON A MOONLESS NIGHT...? WHAT ARE YOU *REALLY* AFTER?
IT'S MY ADORABLE, DETEST-ABLE...
...UNFATH-OMABLE IDIOT OF A DOG.
BINGO.

IS THAT...
TWIK
ピカ
...AN ARM?
THAT IS MINE.
JUST A PIECE...
...OF MY DOG...

TCH...
NO WONDER IT SEEMED TOO EASY.
ZRET
SEEMS A LITTLE CRUEL OF YOU...
...TO STRIKE WITHOUT WARNING... WOULDN'T YOU SAY, INQUISITOR?
KOFF!

DR. FAUST.
THAT VEIL, THE SWORD...
LORENZO CALANDRA? I'VE HEARD TALES OF YOU FROM THE DEMONS.
I SMELLED THIS DEMON'S SCENT COMING FROM YOU.
STAKING YOU OUT WAS THE RIGHT CHOICE...
?!
THE WOUND, IT'S—!
JOHAN-NA!!
FLOP
AN IMMOR-TALITY CURSE.
WHAT A FOOLISH THING.

THIS IS A MISTAKE! SHE'S...
JOHANNA CAN'T BE DR. FAUST...!
FWUP
YOU SEEM A WELL-MEANING LAD TO ME.
NO DOUBT FAUST TRICKED YOU INTO THIS. GET AWAY, FOR YOUR OWN SAFETY.
THE WELL-KNOWN FAIRY TALE ABOUT A GREEDY SCHOLAR.
BUT IT COULDN'T BE...
MOVE AWAY, MARION.
FAIRY TALES CAN ALSO CONTAIN *TRUTH.*
THIS IS A GOOD LESSON FOR YOU. KEEP IT IN MIND.

ARE YOU SAYING YOU'RE THE REAL...?
YOUR DEMON WAS QUARTERED A CENTURY AGO AND HIS POWERS SEALED AWAY.
WHY DO YOU ATTEMPT TO REVIVE HIM NOW?
YOU SHOULD HAVE DIED BACK THEN. WHAT IS YOUR PLOT NOW?
TAK
IT'S VERY, VERY, VERRRY...
...SIMPLE.
THAT'S SIMPLE.

I'M GOING TO CRUSH HIM.
I SIMPLY MUST BURY MY FIST IN THAT MOCKING, POINTLESSLY HANDSOME FACE, AND MAKE HIM GROVEL AND SCRAPE.
CLENCH
SWISH
シュッ
...HUH?
SWIP
AND TO DO THAT, I NEED...
...HIS ENTIRE BODY!
PLIP PLIP
SHLIP
シュル
CLATTER
CLATTER
CLATTER
!

RRP
RIP
RRIP
THE ROCKS ...
SORCERY!
FWAP

GET UP AND MOVE ALREADY, MEPHISTO-PHELES!
THIS WAS *YOUR* GAME TO BEGIN WITH!!

SLICE

TOOK YOU LONG ENOUGH, MEPHISTO. IS IT BECAUSE YOU'RE MISSING YOUR HEAD?
YOU'VE ASSEMBLED THAT MUCH ALREADY?
CREEK
キィ
TUG
MEPHISTO-PHELES...
THAT'S FAUST'S DEMON!

SO LONG, LORENZO.
UNTIL NEXT WE MEET.
ZZSH
...I'D BETTER REPORT IN.
FWAAA

POP
THUD
ARE YOU ALL RIGHT?
GONNA BARF...
SENSORY OVER-LOAD...
HEY!
YOU WERE TRYING TO DO ONE OF YOUR "TRICKS" ON ME, WEREN'T YOU?!
LISTEN.
YOU'LL BE A LOT BETTER OFF FORGETTING ABOUT ALL OF THIS, OKAY?
SORRY FOR GETTING YOU INVOLVED, BUT YOU REALLY OUGHT TO TRUST ME ON THIS ONE.
WHAP

I WASN'T SURE AT FIRST, BUT NOW I AM.
I'M GOING TO FOLLOW YOU!
...WHAT ?!
I'LL LEAVE THE KNOWLEDGE I TAUGHT YOU UNTOUCHED, BUT THE MEMORIES HAVE TO BE TWEAKED...
NO.
SAYS WHO?!
I'M A MONSTER ON THE RUN!
MONSTER, CURSED, WHATEVER— YOU'RE MY TEACHER!
NO ONE ELSE WOULD DO WHAT YOU DID FOR ME.
I WANT TO KEEP LEARNING FROM YOU...

FORGET ABOUT IT.
Geh weg!
CAN'T.

YOU WANT ME TO SPILL THE BEANS ABOUT YOUR BOOK-THIEVING? YOU WANT YOUR POOR MOM TO CRY?!
SHE'LL SAVE MORE MONEY WITHOUT ME! BESIDES, I ALREADY LEFT A LETTER!
HOW STUPID ARE YOU?!
YOU WEREN'T CONFLICTED, YOU WERE PLANNING TO DO THIS FROM THE START!

I'LL BE HELPFUL TO HAVE AROUND THE NEXT TIME THIS HAPPENS!
PLEASE, DOCTOR!
DON'T YOU "DOCTOR" ME!

ON CALL

AFTER FILMING
HE'S GOT TWO: VOICE AND MOTION CAPTURE!
SO MEPHISTO DOESN'T HAVE AN ACTOR?

LET'S PLAY A GAME...
...FAUST.
Ch. 2
IF YOU CAN CATCH ME, YOU WIN.
IF YOU COME TO A STOP, I WIN.
BUT THIS GAME WILL BE DIFFICULT FOR YOU AS A MORTAL.
SO I PROPOSE ...
...A HANDICAP FOR YOU.

Chapter 2:
Waiting in the Forest
...
NOW THAT...
...WAS AN UNPLEASANT DREAM.

WAIT UP, JOHANNA!
BUT I DON'T KNOW THE WAY BACK ANY-MORE...
"WE'RE" NOT GOING ANY-WHERE, IF I CAN HELP IT.
WORRIED? THEN TAKE MY ADVICE AND GO BACK HOME.
YOU STILL HAVEN'T TOLD ME WHERE WE'RE GOING!
I'M GOING TO ONE OF MY LITTLE HIDEOUTS.

DOESN'T SEEM LIKE THERE ARE VERY MANY PEOPLE IN GOOD HEALTH AROUND HERE.
ACHOO!
KOFU!
THERE, MARION.
DEEP IN THOSE WOODS.
OH?
WELL... IT'S ABOUT THAT TIME OF YEAR.
THEY GROW ROUNDWHEAT HERE. THE POLLEN'S GOT A TOXIN THAT HARMS THE NOSE AND THROAT.
FLOWERING SEASON IS HARD ON THOSE MOST AFFECTED BY IT.

I SEEM TO BE FAIRLY CREAKY LATELY...
KRIK
TEACH-ER!
MISS NICO!
THERE'S A VISITOR!

TEACHER!
COMING.
ANOTHER MAGISTRATE COME SEEKING AN EASY BRIBE, I EXPECT...
KRIK
ZSH
ZSH
ZSH
ZSH
ZSH
LOOK HOW BIG YOU ARE...

LONG TIME NO SEE, NICO.
I THOUGHT IT WAS ABOUT THAT TIME.
IT'S SO GOOD TO SEE YOU AGAIN, MOTHER!
TEACHER! I'M GOING INTO TOWN TO SELL MEDICINE!
DON'T LEAVE YET, JOHANNA!
WONDERFUL! IN FACT, YOUR TIMING IS PERFECT.
OH! LOOK HOW SKINNY YOU ARE!
YOU HAVEN'T BEEN EATING PROPERLY, HAVE YOU?
HOW MANY TIMES HAVE I WARNED YOU TO TAKE CARE OF YOURSELF?
KNOCK IT OFF.
ㅎㅡ
SWISH

THEY'RE SO BIG, I HARDLY RECOGNIZE THEM. THEY WERE STILL LITTLE THE LAST TIME I SAW THEM.
MARTINA, KARL...AND BRUNO?
BE CAREFUL, ALL RIGHT?
HAVE A GOOD TRIP!
I WILL!
I'M GOING DOWN TO GET SOME SLEEP BEFORE I WORK.
I'M AFRAID I'M A BIT SHORT ON BLOOD RIGHT NOW.
JUST... GET SOME PROPER REST.
I WILL.
...!
NOT AGAIN, MOTHER!

ER...WHY DO YOU CALL JOHANNA "MOTHER"...?

I'VE BEEN ABANDONED...
UM...
OH? WHO ARE YOU?

SHOULDN'T YOU HAVE A JOB BY NOW?
YOU SEEM TOO BIG TO BE ANOTHER ORPHAN.
I'M... NOT AN ORPHAN...

IT'S FINE...GO AHEAD.
HE'S THE CURIOUS TYPE. YOU CAN TELL HIM IF YOU WANT.

WELL, IF YOU SAY SO, MOTHER...

MOTHER?

MY NAME IS NICO BERNSTEIN, AT YOUR SERVICE.
THE TERM IS LITERAL. I AM THE DAUGHTER OF JOHANNA FAUST.

AHEM... VITO?
DO YOU REMEMBER WHAT I TOLD YOU WHEN I ASSIGNED YOU TO PARTNER WITH LORENZO?
I'M SORRY!
I'M SO SORRY, SIR! I DIDN'T THINK IT WOULD BE THIS BAD...
HONESTLY...
WHAT AM I TO MAKE OF THESE ACCURSED LINES?!
I WARNED YOU THAT HIS ABILITY TO DRAW FACES FROM MEMORY WAS ABYSMAL!

AND LORENZO HAS GONE AHEAD ALREADY?
WELL, WE CAN'T MAKE ARRANGEMENTS NOW...
THEY ONLY ASSIGNED ME TO THAT JOB BECAUSE I KNEW LORENZO!
L-LOOK, I'M JUST A BOOKKEEPER AT THE LIBRARY!
WHAT WAS THE POINT OF HAVING YOU WORK WITH HIM, THEN?!
YOU CAN'T LET HIM GO ON ALONE JUST BECAUSE YOU'RE SCARED!!
YOU MORON!!!
WHAT STILL REMAINS?
AND YOU'RE CERTAIN THAT IT WAS FAUST?
LORENZO SAID THAT THE SMELL WAS THE SAME AS THE PART WE'D JUST FINISHED MOVING— THAT OF MEPHISTO.
THE HEAD, LEFT ARM, AND RIGHT LEG, APPARENTLY.
YES. HE WANTED TO KEEP THE CHASE GOING... SO HE WENT TOWARD THE SILVER FOREST.

AREN'T DEMONS AND HUMANS SUPPOSED TO BE LIKE MERCHANTS AND CUSTOMERS?
THE MAN SELLS HIS SOUL TO THE DEMON...
...AND THE DEMON ACTS AS A SERVANT.
AH... WE'LL NEED TO CONTACT THE REGIONS WHERE THE OTHER PARTS ARE HIDDEN.
BY THE WAY, IT'S NOT OFTEN THAT YOU HEAR ABOUT A DEMON BEING SEALED AWAY.
ESPECIALLY SPLITTING ONE INTO PARTS THAT GET MOVED REGULARLY.
BESIDES, USUALLY THE HUMAN COMMITS THE ACTS, AND THE DEMON SLIPS AWAY. SO WHY IS MEPHISTO BEING—
VITO.
YOU'LL FIND IT EASIER TO FOCUS ON THE JOB IF YOU DON'T ASK THESE QUESTIONS.

SURE THING.
GUESS I'LL GO JOIN THE CHASE FOR LORENZO, THEN.
I WARNED HIM.
BUT HE'S GOING TO GO DIGGING. DAMN THE CURIOSITY OF A RECORD-KEEPER.

KNOWING THE CONNECTION BETWEEN MAN AND DEMON...
...WILL ONLY MAKE THE JOB HARDER.

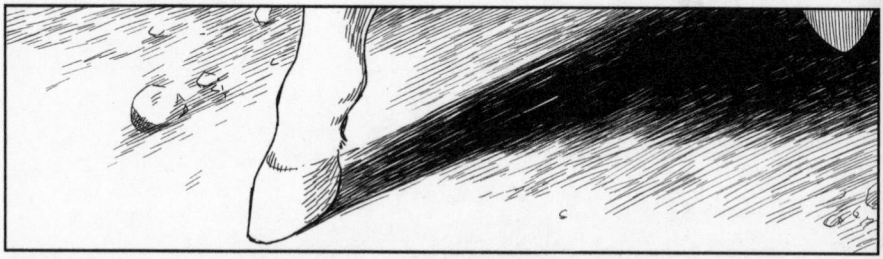

FANCY A LOZENGE, MY LORD?
WE HAVE HERBS TO CURE FEVER AS WELL!

ARE YOU ALL RIGHT, MARTINA?
YOU HAVEN'T LOOKED WELL ALL DAY.
I'M FINE! LET'S HURRY UP AND SELL ALL OF THESE!
CHIRP
CHIRP
I REALLY APPRECIATE YOUR HELP.

YOU SEEM TO BE TAKING LESSONS DIRECTLY FROM MOTHER.

I EXPECT SHE DIDN'T LIKE THAT VERY MUCH.

I RUN A COMBINATION ORPHANAGE AND APOTHECARY, BUT I'M SHORT ON HELP.

OH...

AS SHE TRAVELS, SHE OFTEN PICKS UP ORPHANS WHO SHOW PROMISE.

AFTER ALL, THERE IS NO END TO WAR AND PLAGUE.

SHE *STILL* DOESN'T LIKE IT...

KSHUF

I THINK YOU'LL BE FINE.

SHE'S A SCHOLAR, SO SHE HAS A SOFT SPOT FOR THOSE WHO EXPRESS A DESIRE TO LEARN.

I CAN TELL FROM YOUR EXPRESSION...
...THAT YOU ARE STILL CURIOUS ABOUT ME BEING HER DAUGHTER.
ACK!

HEE-HEE! YOU ARE AN HONEST PERSON.
I'VE ALWAYS GOTTEN SUSPICIOUS LOOKS FROM THE PEOPLE I TELL.
IT'S JUST... JOHANNA LOOKS BARELY OLDER THAN ME AS IT IS.
AND YOU SEEM OLDER THAN HER, TO BOOT.

OH! IS IT BECAUSE...OF THE DEMON'S POWER?
IT CANNOT BE...

...ON ACCOUNT OF THAT SCUM.
I GUESS I STILL DON'T KNOW ANYTHING ABOUT JOHANNA...
...OH! PARDON ME—PLEASE IGNORE THAT.
...
WHAT?
NOTHING.
JUST NOT THE FRUIT OF HER LOINS.
WHISPER
AND I AM ABSOLUTELY MY MOTHER'S CHILD.
SHE MIGHT LOOK LIKE A CHILD NOW, BUT MOTHER IS MOST CERTAINLY GROWN UP.

HISTORY, ASTRONOMY, ALCHEMY, NATURAL HISTORY, MEDICINE...
I KNOW OF HER MANY AREAS OF KNOWLEDGE...
WELL, EVEN THOUGH I HAVEN'T SPENT MUCH TIME WITH HER EITHER...SHE IS FAMILY.
BUT ALL THAT SHE KNOWS WAS THE PRODUCT OF SELF-STUDY.
SHE HAD HELP WITH EXPERI-MENTS AND ACQUIRING RESOURCES.
WITHOUT RELYING ON THE HELP OF A DEMON.
SHE'S TAKEN GREAT PAINS TO MASTER EVERYTHING THAT SHE POSSIBLY CAN.
BUT... ISN'T SHE CONTRACTED TO THAT DEMON— MEPHISTO?
HUH?
...I WONDER WHAT IT WAS SHE WISHED FOR.
THEN...

WHAT DID SHE WANT SO BADLY...
...THAT SHE WOULD HAND OVER HER SOUL FOR IT?
I COULDN'T SAY.
I DO NOT UNDERSTAND EVERY THOUGHT THAT RUNS THROUGH HER HEAD.
ALL THAT'S LEFT ARE WILD STORIES THAT COULD BE TRUE OR FALSE.
THEY TAKE ON A LIFE OF THEIR OWN, AND PAINT HER AS AN INCORRIGIBLE VILLAIN...
...OR A DRIVEN, DEMENTED SCHOLAR.
BUT TO ME...
THE DAY I SAW HER FROM WITHIN THE GLASS...

WHEN I FIRST SAW THAT DELIGHTED SMILE...
...I KNEW THAT I WAS LOOKING UPON THE FACE OF MY MOTHER.
KRIK
"GLASS"?
OH—
?
NICO?
I FOR.
GOT THE.
GRK
GRAK
GEK GEK
GEK
...TIME.

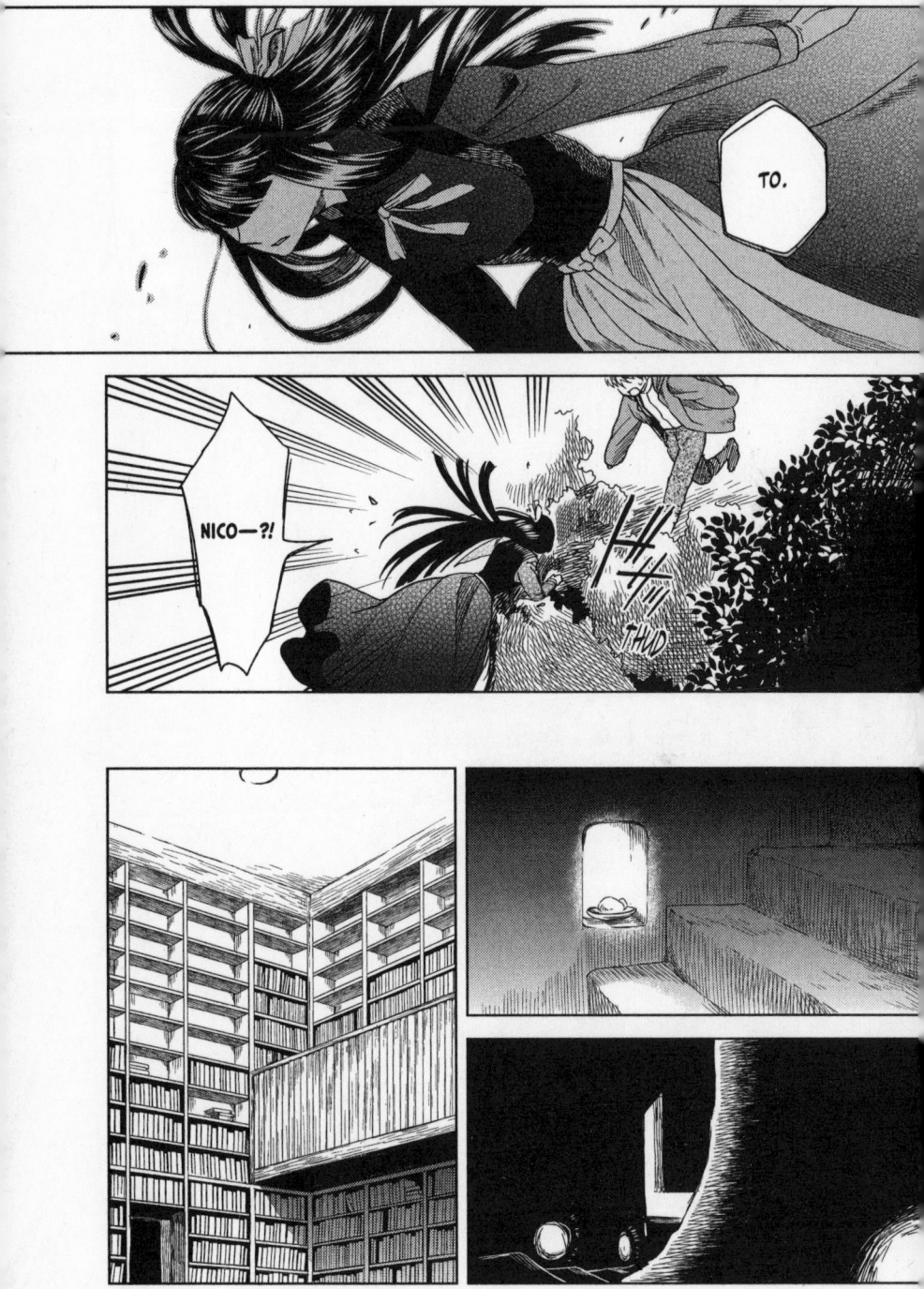
TO.
NICO—?!
THUD

RGH!
HNG!
...SHOULD BE HEALED BY NOW.
ALWAYS TAKES TIME FOR THE INSIDES TO ATTACH.
CREAK
THERE.

STUPID HANDICAP MEPHISTO GAVE ME.
SLIP
OH?
ZWLIP
DAMN... LOST MORE, HAVE I?
I HATE BEING SO SHORT.

THUMP
!
NGK!

...WHAT ARE YOU DOING?
EARLIER, YOU WOULDN'T BOTHER TO HELP UNLESS I WAS ON THE VERGE OF DYING.
IS THIS JUST BECAUSE YOU GOT YOUR ARM BACK?
I WON'T GIVE YOU THE SATIS-FACTION OF WINNING.

JOHAN-NA!
COME QUICK! IT'S NICO!!
I'M ON...
...MY WAY.

JOHANNA!
WHAT... WHAT IS WITH HER BODY? WHY DID SHE COLLAPSE ...?
YES.
NICO.
ARE YOU IN THERE?
NEEDS MAINTE-NANCE.
SHE'S DUE.
パシャン
SPLISH
THEY SPEAK AND ACT ALL OF THEIR OWN VOLITION, BUT BEING MANMADE, THEY REQUIRE CHECKUPS AND SERVICING.
IN A LAND TO THE WEST, THEY HAVE DOLLS THAT CAN MOVE ON THEIR OWN.
MAINTE-NANCE?

YOU HAVE A KNACK FOR BEING PRESENT AT INTERESTING EVENTS.
CLOSING PSEUDO-SPINE GATE ALPHA-1.
ALPHA-2.
ALPHA-3.
CHAK
CHK
KRIK...
THERE.
I'M GOING TO CLOSE THE PLUGS ON YOUR NERVE TRANSMIT-TERS.
CIRCUIT F-12.
LOOKS GOOD.
...
PERFORMING EXTRACTION.

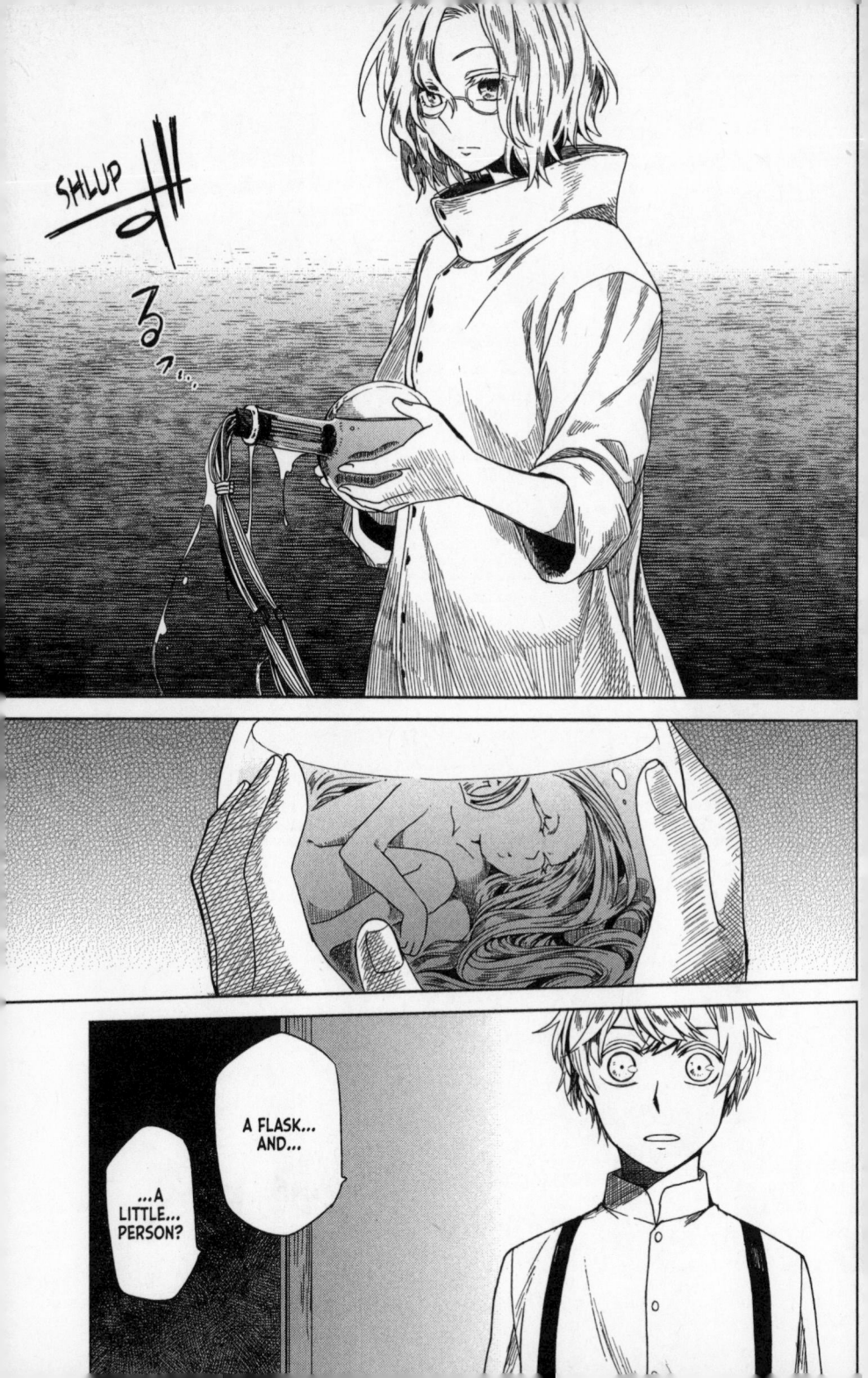
SHLUP
A FLASK... AND...
...A LITTLE... PERSON?

IT'S A HOMUNCULUS.
A PRODUCT OF ALCHEMY.
BLUP
IT CAN ONLY LIVE WITHIN THIS FLASK.
IT CAN'T DO MUCH LIKE THIS, SO THE DOLL BODY ALLOWS IT TO MOVE AROUND.
SPLISH
IT HAS BEEN A LONG TIME... SINCE I USED THIS VOICE.
GOOD. CHANGING TO QUARTZ PREVENTED ANY DEGRADATION.
SORRY ABOUT THIS.
I WANT TO MAKE IT SO THAT YOU CAN VENTURE OUTSIDE SOON...
I'M HAPPY JUST LIKE THIS.

MAYBE SO, BUT...
...
...
THERE'S SO MUCH I WANT TO ASK.
BUT THE WORDS WON'T COME.
IT'S NOT AT ALL LIKE THE FAIRY TALES.
SHE LOVES HER CHILDREN.
SHE'S BEEN LOOKING FOR HER DEMON FOR A HUNDRED YEARS.
SHE'S BRILLIANT AND KNOWLEDGEABLE.
WHAT A MYSTERIOUS PERSON...
...THERE.

THAT WRAPS UP THE PRIMARY MAINTE-NANCE.
JUST DON'T GET TOO ACTIVE UNTIL I'VE GONE OVER YOUR JOINTS.
OKAY.
TEACH-ER!
MISS NICO!!
IT'S MARTINA, MISS NICO!
OH, YOU'RE BA—

MOVE.
SHE JUST COLLAPSED. SHE'S GOT A FEVER AND TERRIBLE PAINS.
WHAT'S THE MATTER, MARTINA?
...!
ER, NO, WE'RE OUT AT THE MOMENT, BUT...
OH! DO YOU THINK—?
YES.
AND REDCHAIN PETALS.
GOT ANY OF THOSE TWO IN STOCK?
ROOT OF TRILEAF DAFFODIL.

IT'S A "SEED."

STUNT PRACTICE

BLOOPER
CUUUT!
SOR-
RY!!
I'M
SORRY
!!!
I'M...
FINE
...

FZZT
ARE YOU REALLY GOING TO HAND OVER THAT EAR OF WHEAT?
THAT PARASITIC THING... THAT IS CERTAIN TO LEAD TO MANY DEATHS?
CH. 5
...
THEY'RE SUFFERING A FAMINE.
IT'S BETTER THAN ENTIRE TOWNS DYING OUT.
...I SEE.
TOK
BUTT OUT OF THIS, MEPHISTO.
OR DID YOU JUST WANT TO RUN A LITTLE EXPERIMENT?

Chapter 3:
That Belongs to Me

LISTEN TO ME, MARION.
IF YOU RUN OUT BEHIND THE HOUSE, YOU'LL EVENTUALLY COME ACROSS A STREAM.
THERE SHOULD BE A NUMBER OF PINE TREES THERE WITH WHITE NEEDLES.
FIND A DAFFODIL AT THE BASE OF THOSE TREES AND PULL IT OUT, ROOTS AND ALL.
THEN PICK ALL THE RED VINE FLOWERS YOU CAN FIND ON THE TRUNK.
...“SEED“?
NO, YOU REST...
I'LL GO TOO, MOTHER.

ALL RIGHT, FINE. GO ON.
WE ARE!
THE REST OF YOU, ARRANGE A BED AND HEAT UP SOME WATER.
JOHANNA!
WHAT DO YOU MEAN, "SEED"? WHAT KIND OF SEED?
WE'LL JUST HAVE TO MAKE DO WITH WHAT'S ON HAND FOR NOW.
GREAK
...

LET'S GET MOVING. WE'VE GOT TO HURRY!
RIGHT!
PLEASE GO ON AHEAD WITHOUT ME, MARION.
BUT WHY IS HE HERE...?
A PRIEST? HE'S GOT A SWORD...
AN INQUISITOR?
IT SEEMS LIKE TROUBLE HAS COME LOOKING FOR US. I'LL TAKE CARE OF IT.

!
THAT'S THE MAN WE MET BEFORE...
WELCOME, MY LORD.
WHAT BRINGS YOU TO THIS REMOTE PLACE?
TEP
NICO! HE'S AFTER JOH—
I KNOW! JUST GO!
...!
ANY IDEAS ABOUT THE SOURCE?
I SMELLED A WICKED ODOR EMANATING FROM HERE.
THE STENCH OF A DEMON.

...MY LORD?
DO YOU MIND IF I LOOK INSIDE?
SWISH
DEMON ...?
I'VE NEVER SEEN SUCH A TERRIFYING THING IN MY LIFE.
ALL THE MORE REASON TO ENSURE THEIR SAFETY...
YOU MUSN'T! OUR CHILDREN ARE BEDRIDDEN WITH SICKNESS INSIDE!
I'M AFRAID YOU WILL CATCH WHAT THEY CARRY!

YOU DON'T HAVE...
...A HUMAN BODY, DO YOU?
KRK
WHAT DID YOU ...?!
TEP
SSH
SWISH

KCHING
SWISH
YOU MOVE WELL.
BUT...
UMF
カタカタ...
KRRKK
!!
SHISH
WHUD

YOU HAVE A WILL.
...A DOLL?
NO, NOT QUITE.
WHY DO YOU HIDE IT?

WHIFF
WHAT DO YOU THINK YOU'RE DOING...
ZSH
...TO MY DAUGHTER?
HUH?!

FAUST...
ZSHF
ZSHF
SHF
HF!
HF!
HF!
DO YOU KNOW HOW WHEAT PROPA-GATES?
OF COURSE I DO. YOU JUST PLANT THE GRAIN SEEDS.

ROUND-WHEAT IS A STRAIN THAT OCCASIONALLY PRODUCES MUTATED POLLEN.
YES, IF THEY'RE BEING CULTIVATED BY HUMAN BEINGS.
BUT WHEN THEY FLOWER NATURALLY, THE POLLEN SPREADS THROUGH THE AIR TO FERTILIZE THE GRAIN AND PRODUCE KERNELS.
ONCE IT KILLS THE HOST, IT GROWS BY ABSORBING THE BODY'S NUTRIENTS.
AND THIS MUTATED POLLEN "SEED" ENTERS THE BODY OF ANIMALS AND TAKES ROOT.
THE SEEDS HARDLY EVER BLOOM.
IT'S MORE COMMON FOR THEM TO COMPLICATE A SEASONAL COLD AND CAUSE DEATH.
TH... THEN—!
YOU THINK EVERYONE IN THIS VILLAGE IS—?
EUGH...

SCRITCH
SCRITCH
AND ONCE A BODY IS BURIED, THE SEEDS DIE WITHOUT SUNLIGHT.
CLINK
CLIK
HOW DO YOU KNOW THIS STUFF, JOHANNA...?
I HAD ORIGINALLY RECEIVED IT FROM A FELLOW SCHOLAR...
THUNK
WHY...
WHY WOULD YOU HAVE SUCH A DANGEROUS THING?!
BECAUSE I WAS THE ONE WHO BROUGHT THE PLANT TO THIS TOWN.

...
IF THE DEATH OF ONE OR TWO COULD ENSURE THE SURVIVAL OF DOZENS OR HUNDREDS...
...WOULD YOU NOT MAKE THAT CHOICE?
I...I CAN'T...
...MAKE THAT DECISION...
MMF
...!

JUST GO AND GET THE PLANTS.
IF WE'RE NOT QUICK, SHE'LL DIE.
...!
ZSHH
HUFF!
HUFF!
I WONDER...
...IF SHE BLAMES HERSELF FOR THIS...

FSHHH
ア ア ア...
THAT'S THE STREAM...
FSHH
ガァァ...
OKAY, PINE WITH WHITE NEEDLES.
CRIK
ROOTS.
AND.
TRUNK.

THAT'S IT.
RIP
IT'S TOO LATE TO TAKE MY TIME NOW!
HMF
GRRK
THERE'S A PARTICULAR PLANT WHOSE TOXIN BURNS THE SEED'S ROOTS.
THAT MEANS IT'S POISONOUS, SO PICK IT CAREFULLY.

MMF
WUBB
じわ…
TST
OUCH...!
ZSH
SHUK
SHUK
ZSH!
SHRIK
NNG
...THERE!

MOTH-ER!
DON'T PUSH YOUR-SELF TOO HARD!
GRK
KRIK
CHIK
AH!
SHING
ZRMM
PWA
ZWURP

FOOL!
HOW AM I TO PROTECT MY CHILDREN WITHOUT "PUSHING TOO HARD"?
RIP
CLOTHING
...!
KREK

HMF
SO YOU'RE NOT VANISHING THIS TIME.
WHAT IS THIS "DAUGHTER" BUSINESS?
HMM?
WHY DOESN'T SHE FLEE?
IT MEANS THAT SHE IS MY TRUST-WORTHY DAUGHTER...
...WHO IS TOO GOOD FOR THE LIKES OF ME.
ZUNK
FWOSH
CRAKK

GSHK
WE'RE TENDING TO THE SICK.
FSH
THUNK
SO THIS...
...IS PAY-BACK.
I WAS JUST PASSING BY, AND DECIDED TO HELP THEM OUT OF THE KINDNESS OF MY HEART.
I WISH YOU'D FOCUS ON THAT PART.

MARION?
SICK? YOU LIE...
IT'S NOT A LIE!
IT'S NOT A LIE.
THERE'S A GIRL INSIDE...
...AT DEATH'S DOOR.
HUFF!
PLEASE... WE NEED HELP.
SO LET HER GO...

THANK YOU.
I SUPPOSE I PUSHED MYSELF TOO HARD...
GRRG
MY BODY WON'T MOVE.
CANK
IT'S ALL RIGHT.
YOU'LL HAVE TO STAY THERE FOR NOW, NICO! SORRY!

YOU CAN CERTAINLY AFFORD TO IGNORE HER FOR A LITTLE BIT LONGER.
YOU LEFT HER ALONE FOR A HUNDRED YEARS.
WE'RE NOT GOING TO KILL YOU.
RRGH
I CAN'T MOVE HER.
WHY DO YOU OBEY FAUST?
I DO NOT...
...OBEY HER.
I SUPPOSE I MIGHT GET DESTROYED.
OH, THOSE POOR CHILDREN...

IS SHE CONTROLLING YOU?
...YOU DON'T GET IT.
I MADE ALL OF MY OWN DECISIONS.
ANY REGRETS OR DOUBTS ARE MINE ALONE.
I MADE THE DECISION TO HELP HER, AWKWARD THOUGH SHE MAY BE.
SHE BROUGHT ME LIFE, INCOMPLETE OR NOT.

IT IS NOT ANYONE'S FAULT. I MADE THE DECISION.
I AM THE SUM OF MY OWN CHOICES, AND I BELONG TO ME.

THAT IS A GOOD WAY TO THINK.
MAY GOD BESTOW HIS BLESSING UPON THE PATH YOU HAVE CHOSEN.

SST
BUT WHEN THE TREATMENT IS OVER, I WILL ARREST MY TARGET.
IF MEPHISTO IS RESTORED TO NORMAL, HUMANKIND WILL SUFFER—
GONK
FUBP FUBP
KAW
KAW
IN RECOGNITION OF YOUR STRENGTH OF WILL...
...AND FOR THE SAKE OF THE SICK, REAL OR FICTIVE, I WILL TURN A BLIND EYE.

...OR ANYTHING ELSE IN LIFE.
OF THAT...
NO GUAR-ANTEE.
ISN'T SHE SAFE NOW?
AND NOW...WE WAIT.
BRINGING THAT DANGEROUS PLANT HERE.
REGRET WHAT?
YOU DON'T REGRET IT, JOHANNA?
CRK

I DON'T.

...OH.

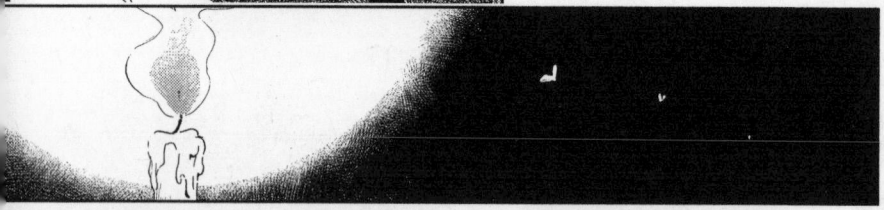

CAN YOU SPARE SOME OF THOSE EARS FOR ME?
WE'VE HAD A SPATE OF COLD SUMMERS. THE HARVESTS HAVE BEEN LACKING.

PLEASE, I BEG OF YOU.
CLINK
ガラン

...OF THE LAND OF OUR ANCESTORS' SWEAT AND TOIL.
IT IS STILL A BETTER FATE THAN THE UTTER RUIN...
BUT AT SOME POINT, THEY WILL COME BACK TO HARM YOU.
I TOLD YOU EARLIER.
THESE WILL TAKE root WHEREVER YOU SCATTER THEM.
YOU SURE?
IT WILL ONLY CAUSE THEM TO WORRY.
...I WILL NOT TELL THE OTHERS ABOUT THAT.
AND YOU LOVE A GOOD EXPERI-MENT, DON'T YOU?
A MUTANT WHEAT THAT SETS ROOT IN THE FLESH IT DEVOURS!
YOU MAY HAVE SET UP A NICE LITTLE EXPERI-MENT.
ALL'S WELL THAT ENDS WELL, RIGHT?

HOW-EVER ...
THEY'RE GOOD FUN.
...I DO.
GRMP
...IT'S ONLY BECAUSE I CAN TEST A PROPER SOLUTION.

THAT WAS THE BEST CHOICE I HAD AT THE TIME.
I DON'T REGRET IT, AND I WON'T FEEL BAD ABOUT IT.
I'M GOING TO FIND THE ANSWER.
DON'T ASSUME THAT I'LL CRUMBLE THAT EASILY...
...DEMON.
VERY GOOD, FAUST.
SWISH
THAT IS THE MASTER WHOM I KNOW SO WELL.

HOW MANY TIMES HAVE I RECALLED THAT SMILE?
AND IT'S JUST AS CREEPY EVERY SINGLE TIME.
I GAVE HIM A LITTLE BOP AND HE STOPPED TALKING.
SO I WENT AND DUMPED HIM OUTSIDE OF TOWN.
HE SHOULDN'T CHASE US AGAIN. IT'S FINE.
GRUNK
GRUNK
?
WAIT, WHERE'S THE GUY, NICO?
...
KRK
MOTHER! HOW IS MARTINA'S CONDITION?
THUMP
SHE'S STABLE NOW.
...
I SEE.
WELL, IF YOU SAY SO...
SWAY
...I'LL TAKE YOUR WORD FOR...

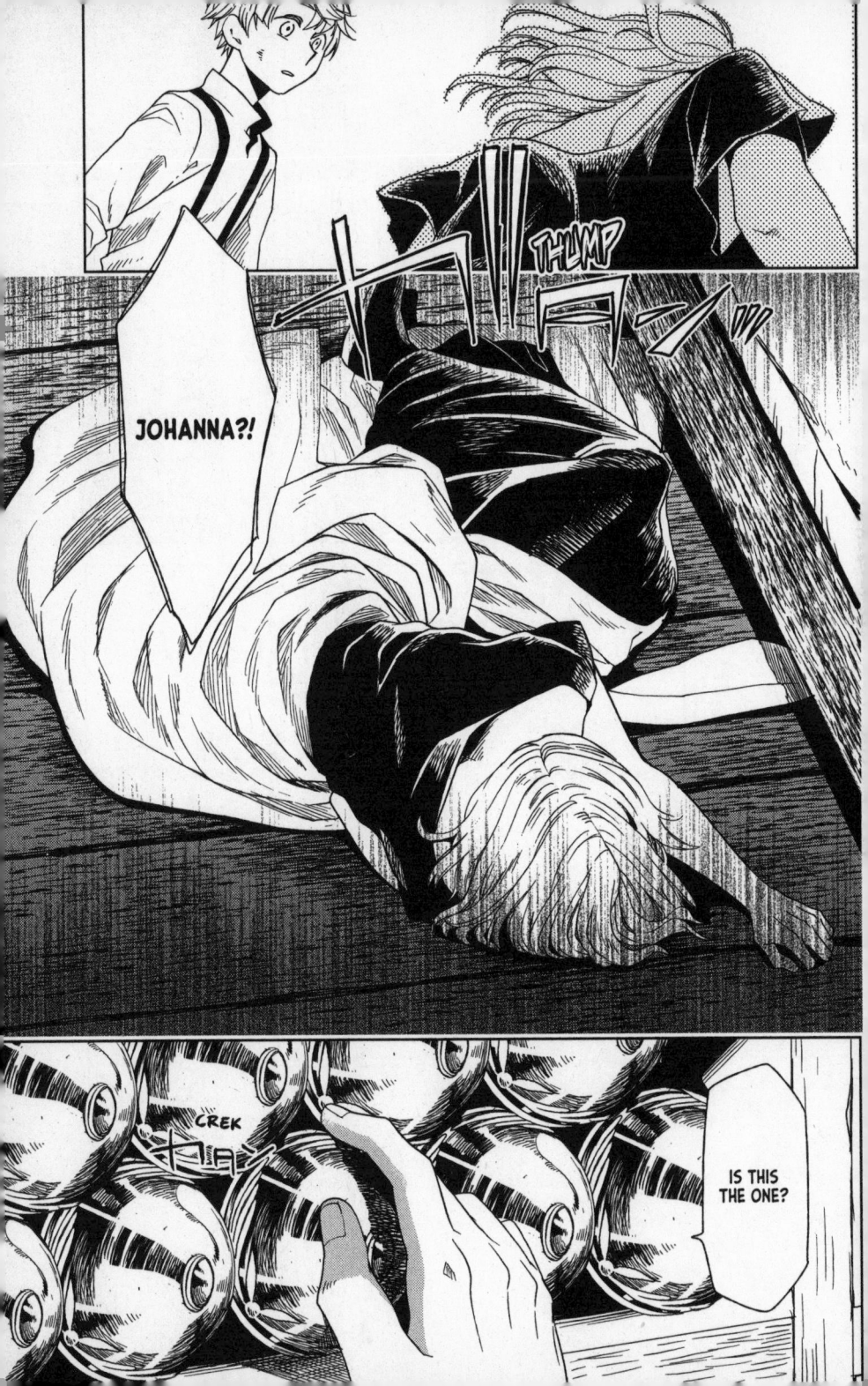
THUMP
JOHANNA?!
CREK
IS THIS THE ONE?

PONK
THE TRIAL OF THE DEMON MEPHISTO-PHELES...
EASIER TO FIND THAN I THOUGHT.
HMM? JUST ONE CHARGE?
FWIP
SHWIP
LET'S SEE... CHARGES ARE...
WELL, GIVEN THE SEVERITY OF THE SEALING METHODS, HE MUST HAVE DONE SOMETHING UNSPEAKABLE. FOR THEM TO HUSH IT UP LIKE THIS...
THE CRIME OF PLACING AN UNWARRANTED IMMORTALITY CURSE...
...UPON THE DEAD...?
TO BE CONTINUED IN VOL. 2

FAMILY CASTING

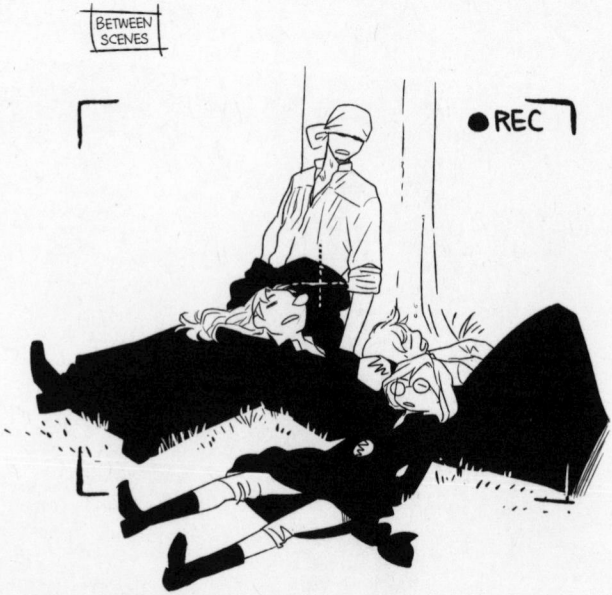
BETWEEN SCENES
REC

The Invisible Museum

Divorce Application
Name
Husband

OH, BOY.
VERY SOON NOW.

The
Invisible
Museum

YOU IN THE MARKET?
YUP.
PART-TIME JOBS?
I WANNA GET THE HELL OUT OF MY HOUSE, NOW. I NEED MONEY.
YOU'RE IN A ROUGH SPOT, HUH?
PART-TIMERS WANTED
PART-TIME WORK
SEEKING PART-TIMERS
WANT LAID-BACK WORK, LOW HOURS?
PART-TIME BEEF BOWLS
TEMPORARY AVAILABLE
PART-TIME JOBS
AHH, GOTCHA.
BUT THAT MONEY COULD DRY UP BEFORE I GRADUATE.
I GUESS SO.
HEY, WHATEVER. DIVORCE IS A FACT OF LIFE NOW.
YOU DON'T MINCE WORDS, YUKIMURA.
DON'T YOU GET CHILD SUPPORT FROM YOUR DAD, THOUGH?

HUH?

YUKI-MURA ...?
GUESS I DITCHED HER SOME-WHERE.
WAS THIS HUGE BUILDING ALWAYS HERE?
JUST A PEEK WON'T HURT.
GALLERY OPEN
ARE THEY HAVING AN EXHIBITION OR SOME-THING?

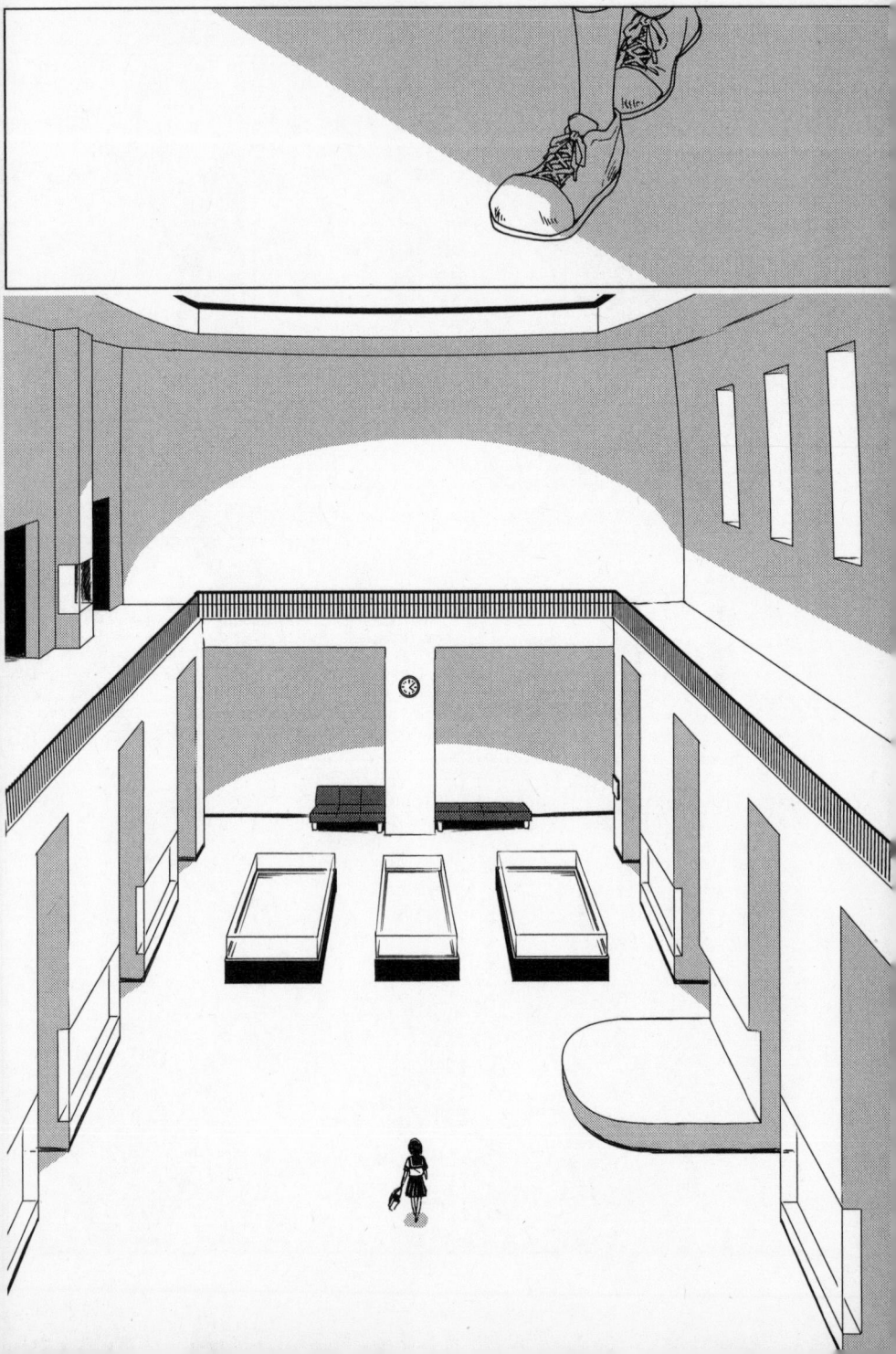

NOTHING HERE.

THERE ARE PLATFORMS AND CASES, THOUGH.

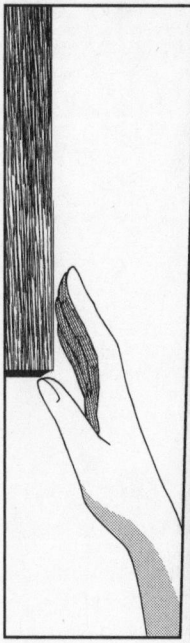

A WOODEN BOX...FOR DISPLAYING SPECIMENS?
THERE'S NOTHING IN IT.

...LIKE THEY JUST BROKE FREE AND ESCAPED.

CORRECT.

YIKES, HE'S CRAZY.
UH.
OKAY.
UMM.
I'M SORRY FOR JUST LETTING MYSELF IN.

THE SIGN SAID WE WERE OPEN. IT'S PERFECTLY ALL RIGHT.

WHAT WAS IN THERE...
...MANAGED TO ESCAPE.

UH... RIGHT.
WHAT DO YOU MEAN, AND WHO ARE YOU?
...AND MORE LIKE AN *EXHIBITION SAMPLE.* WE DON'T DO HUMANS, THOUGH.
HOWEVER, YOU SEEM LESS LIKE A CUSTOMER ...

STARE
じろじろ
IT'S BEEN QUITE A WHILE SINCE WE'VE HAD A VISITOR.

I AM THE DIRECTOR OF THIS MUSEUM.

MUSEUM? BUT THERE'S NOTHING HERE.
YOU JUST CAN'T SEE IT YET.

WHAT WE HAVE HERE ARE THOSE WHO HIDE AND REST BECAUSE THEY DO NOT LIKE TO BE SEEN.

HA HA HA. I FIND YOUR ATTITUDE TO BE BRACING.
UM... ARE YOU... OKAY?
ARE YOU SLEEP-TALKING?
CURIOUS EYES, GREEDY EYES, DIRTY FINGERS.
OUR EXHIBITS HAVE GROWN TIRED OF SUCH THINGS.
SO IT IS PROPER THAT YOU CANNOT SEE THEM.
ASAKI-SAN?
IWANAVI
2014 JUNE
JOBS NEAR YOU!
CREEEP
じり じり
WH—
WHEN DID YOU...
THE WISDOM OF AGE.
AH!
IWA
AS

DO YOU NEED MONEY, ASAKI-SAN? YOU DON'T SEEM LIKE THE TYPE TO BE DRAWN TO A LIFE OF LUXURY.
GIVE! THAT! BACK!!
IF YOU WANT THE LISTING BACK, I'LL GIVE IT TO YOU.
BUT HOW ABOUT A JOB...
...HERE AT THE INVISIBLE MUSEUM?

THE LOOK FITS YOU LIKE A GLOVE.
WHAT IS THIS? SOME KIND OF HAZING RITUAL?
THE BEST PLACE TO START IS WITH THE LOOK.

THERE WAS A BUTTERFLY IN THAT DISPLAY CASE.
BUTTER-FLY?

IT WAS SUCH A PERFECT SPECIMEN THAT IT'D BEEN SOLD TIME AND TIME AGAIN. SO DESIRABLE THAT IT PROMPTED QUARRELS.
EVENTUALLY IT GREW SO TIRED OF THE ATTENTION THAT IT WENT INVISIBLE TO AVOID IT.
THAT WAS HOW IT LANDED HERE AT THE MUSEUM.

WHY?
I'M THE DIREC-TOR.
THAT'S NOT AN ANSWER.
ALL I CAN TELL YOU IS THAT I WAS BORN THIS WAY.
...

IF IT'S INVISIBLE, HOW DID IT GET TRANSPORTED HERE?
I CAN SEE BETTER THAN MOST.

THIS MUSEUM HAS A SPECIAL QUALITY.
FOR THE SAKE OF ITS SUBJECTS, IT DOES NOT LET IN THE AVERAGE, CURIOUS BROWSER.
AND YET YOU WERE ABLE TO COME INSIDE, YOU SEE?
THEN WHY DID YOU LET IT ESCAPE? SURELY YOU COULD CATCH IT YOURSELF.
NO, IT'S FINE.
LET ME GUESS— YOU CAN'T ACTUALLY SEE IT AFTER ALL!
DON'T WORRY, IT HASN'T LEFT THE MUSEUM.
AND, WELL, THIS OLD BODY OF MINE IS TOO FEEBLE TO CATCH A FLUTTERING BUTTERFLY.
ACTUALLY, I DROPPED THE BOX WHEN I WAS DOING MAINTENANCE.
CRAKK
AH!
...
...SO I CANNOT SAY IF IT WILL APPEAR AS A BUTTERFLY TO YOU, TOO.
...YOUR EYES ARE DIFFERENT FROM MINE...
HOW-EVER ...
WELL, GREAT.

I'VE BEEN NABBED BY A REAL WEIRD BUILDING AND PERSON.

JOLT

TEP
TEP
TEP

GUESS I CAN PLAY ALONG WITH THIS OLD MAN'S GAME.
LEAKS OF PERSONAL INFORMATION ARE NO JOKE THESE DAYS, THOUGH...
SIGH

THIS PLACE IS SPOOKY...

IT'S...
...A SHADOW. SWIMMING.
ばくんっ CHOMP
WHAT IS THAT ...?
IT... ATE SOME-THING?
MNCH もぐ
しゅるっ SHLUUP
AH.

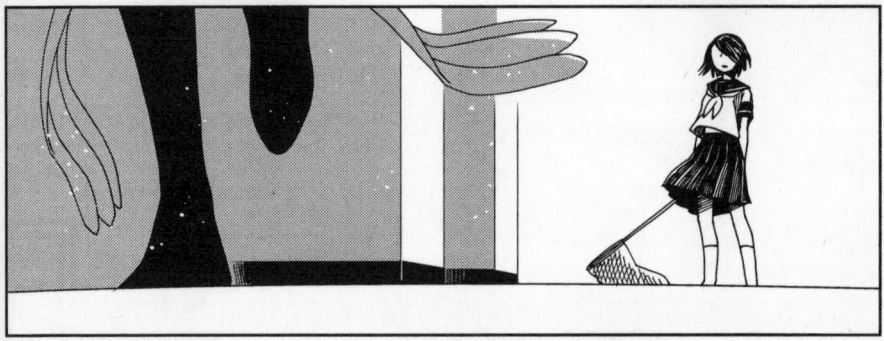

PLEASE KEEP COMING BACK UNTIL YOU CATCH IT!
WELL, AS LONG AS YOU'RE PAYING... SURE.
CLIK

AND NO SHAPES OR SHADOWS AFTER THAT..

WAS THAT SUPPOSED TO BE... THE BUTTERFLY?

C'MON, LET'S GET YOU TO YOUR BED.
MOM.
CLICK
カチッ
I'M HOME.
WHY DID I GET STUCK WITH YUME AND NOT YUSUKE?
WHY DID IT HAVE TO BE YOU?
WHY...
MOM?
VERY SOON NOW.
YU-SUKE...
YUSUKE.

SWISH
ひらり
WHOOSH
WHOOSH
SWISH
ひらり
HOW GOES IT?
HUFF
HUFF
WHEEZE!
WHEEZE!
HUFF
HUFF
WHEEZE!
WHEEZE!

NOWHERE! NOWHERE AT ALL!
ITS WINGS ARE RUSTY AFTER BEING PINNED DOWN AND GAWKED AT FOR SO LONG.
WELL... FEEL FREE TO PLAY WITH IT FOR AS LONG AS YOU LIKE.
WHAT IS THAT THING, SOME KIND OF DEMON?
YOU DON'T HAVE MUCH STAMINA FOR A CHILD.
SPEAK FOR YOURSELF, GRAMPS!
THIS ISN'T... WHAT I SIGNED UP FOR.
I REQUEST A PAY RAISE.
YOU'RE ACTUALLY MUCH TOUGHER THAN YOU LOOK, AREN'T YOU?

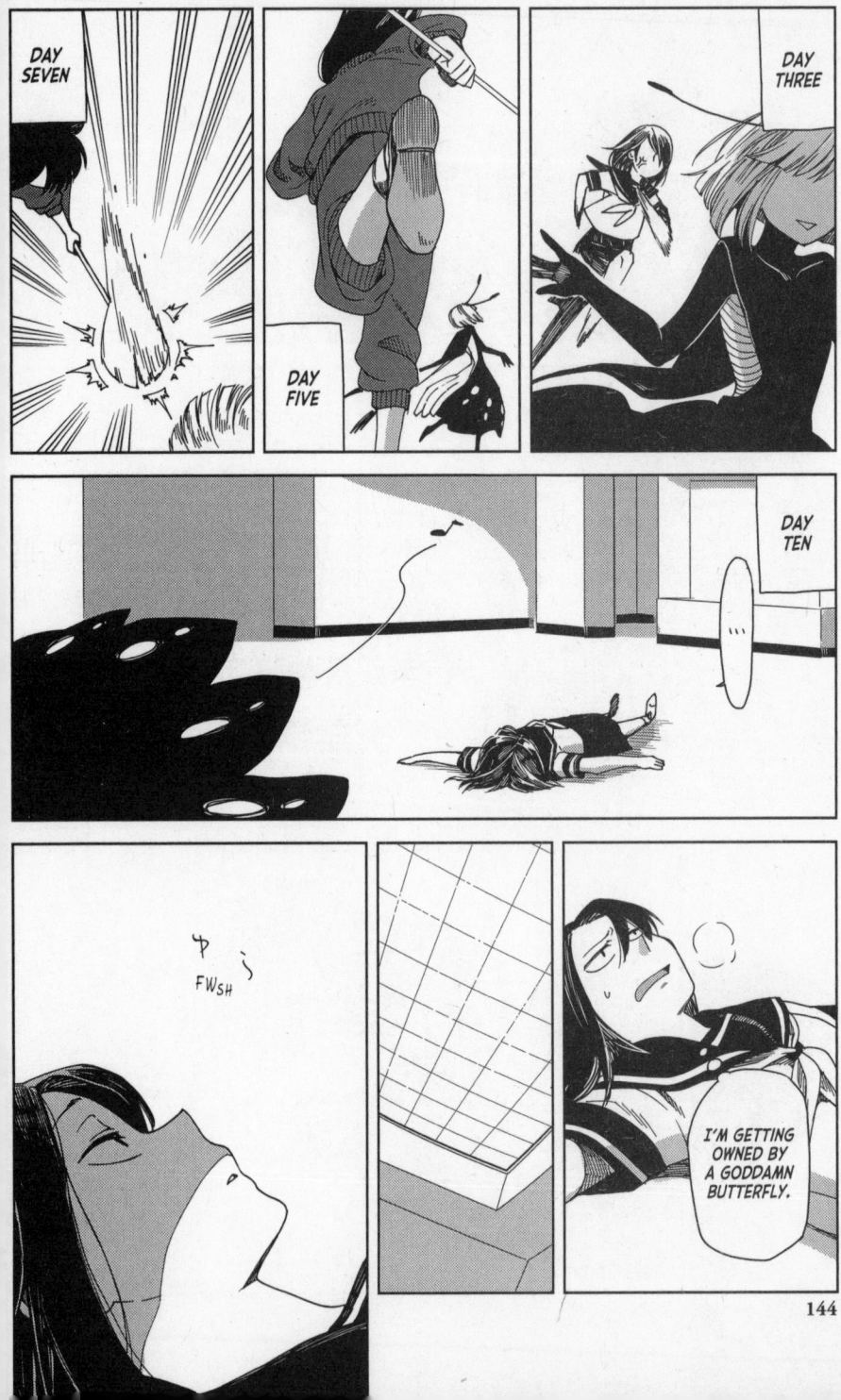
DAY SEVEN
DAY FIVE
DAY THREE
DAY TEN
...
FWSH
I'M GETTING OWNED BY A GODDAMN BUTTERFLY.

IT'S LIKE I'M ON...
...THE RIVERBED, LOOKING UP.

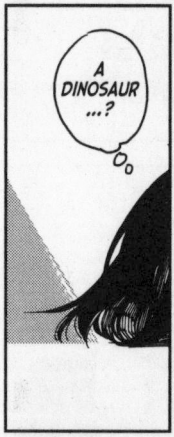
A DINOSAUR ...?

WHAT IS THAT THING?
LOOKS LIKE A GATOR.

MY BROTHER'S SMART AND CAPABLE AND CLEARLY THE ONE MY PARENTS FAVORED.
I COULDN'T STAND THE WAY I ALWAYS GOT COMPARED TO HIM.
I'M NOT VERY PRETTY, I'M NOT CONSIDERATE, AND I'M NOT HELPFUL.
...AND I HAVE NO STAMINA, EITHER.
THAT'S WHAT I WANT TO DO.
YOU WANTED TO DISAPPEAR TOO, HUH?

SO IF THEY DON'T WANT ME...
...I'LL GO AWAY.

HEE HEE

DAMN!

ひょいっ
ZWIP
WHACK
バキッ
YAH!

SUCH COM-PARISONS HAPPEN...
...AT A VERY DEEP LEVEL FOR ALL LIFE.

EVERY-ONE AND EVERY-THING...
...IS INEVITABLY INVOLVED IN THE ACT OF COMPARISON.
FOR AS LONG AS YOU LIVE.
THE MORE BEAUTI-FUL.
THE STRON-GER.
THE MORE BRILLIANT.
BLINK
BUT...

CLANK
カラン
CHOMP

YOU CAN'T...
...EAT IT.
IF ANYTHING ELSE WILL DO, YOU CAN EAT ME.
BUT NOT THIS ONE.

SLUMP
HOOOO BOY...
I THOUGHT THAT WAS IT FOR ME.
WHA—
WHA—
WHA—
HMPH
BECAUSE THE DIRECTOR PROBABLY WOULD'VE BEEN PISSED IF I LET YOU GET EATEN. PLUS...
WHY DID YOU PROTECT ME...?
YOU WERE BEAUTIFUL.

MORE BEAUTIFUL THAN ANYTHING I'VE EVER SEEN.
IF THAT'S WHAT YOU THINK...
...THEN I'M SATISFIED.
SWISH
...OH.

LIVING THINGS CANNOT HELP BUT MAKE COMPARISONS.

KTUNK
BUT...

YOU MEAN... YOU'LL GO BACK?
TO CONTINUE FROM EARLIER...
HUH?

...NOT ALL THINGS HAVE THE SAME KIND OF EYES.

I SHALL PRAY THAT THE ONE TO CHOOSE YOU...
...WILL COME ALONG TO FIND YOU SOON...
OOOH.
LOOK AT THIS.

WHAT BEAUTIFUL WINGS.
IT'S SO BIG. PERHAPS A MUTATION?
IN-CRED-IBLE.
IT'S GOR-GEOUS.
THIS SHOULD GO FOR QUITE A LOT.
IT'S A RARE SPECIES, AND A HUGE INDIVIDUAL.
I'M SURE SOME ECCEN-TRIC WILL PAY OUT THE NOSE FOR IT.
OH. I GET IT.
ALL THE BUTTERFLY WANTED...
...WAS FOR SOMEONE TO SAY...
...THAT IT WAS BEAUTIFUL...

AWAKE NOW?

HE SEEMS TO HAVE RETURNED, AND NOW I CAN FINALLY HAND HIM TO THE CLIENT.
SEE? ISN'T HE BEAUTI-FUL?

...DIREC-TOR!
YOU HAD PASSED OUT.

...YES.

WAIT.
HE?
YES, HE.

EVEN I DON'T KNOW WHEN IT FIRST CAME HERE.
BUT THE SHADOW WILL EAT THOSE WHO, WITH ALL OF THEIR BEING, WISH TO DISAPPEAR.
HE SEEMS TO HAVE CHANGED HIS MIND DURING HIS PURSUIT, AND RE-TREATED.
THAT WAS A MALE?!
IT'S THE MALE BUTTERFLIES WHO ARE MORE BEAUTIFUL THAN THE FEMALES. THEY VIE FOR ATTENTION THAT WAY.
THAT'S CRAZY...
OH, AND THE SHADOW ON THE CEILING.
WHAT IS THAT THING?
IT'S SOME-THING OF A RESCUE DEVICE.
ASAKI-SAN...
THERE ARE MANY PROBLEMS THAT ARISE WHEN A PERSON DIS-APPEARS.
YOU WERE LISTENING IN? THAT'S CREEPY.
IT'S QUIET HERE. YOU CAN'T HELP BUT HEAR THINGS.
BUT YOU ARE YOU, NO MATTER WHO YOU'RE COMPARED TO. AND THERE'S NOTHING WRONG WITH THAT.

THE POINT IS...

AND YOU WON'T EVEN DENY IT...
YOU ARE VERY PERCEPTIVE, MY DEAR.
IT'S SHALLOW. YOUR HEART'S NOT IN IT.
WHY NOT?
THAT'S NOT HELPFUL.

YOU'RE JUST STUBBORN, THE SAME WAY A MALE BUTTERFLY IS.

AND THAT IS WHY THE THING IN THE CEILING DIDN'T EAT YOU.
YOU DON'T WANT TO ACKNOWLEDGE THE HUMILIATION OF YOUR PARENTS CHOOSING YOUR BROTHER OVER YOU.

YOUR DESIRE IS A CHILDISH ESCAPE.

HFH.
NO COUNTER-ARGU-MENT?
I'VE GOT NOTHING TO DEBATE WITH.
OUCH, OUCH.
BONK
BONK
OOH, YOU'RE SULKING.
BUT TRY TO SEE THINGS FROM MY PERSPECTIVE, AS THE GIRL WHO'S LEFT BEHIND WITH THE DRUNKEN MOTHER WHO CAN'T GET OVER THE DIVORCE, YOU CREEPY WEIRDO!
YES, YOU'RE RIGHT! I'M A CHILD. I'M JEALOUS.
BUT IT WOULD BE A WASTE TO DISAPPEAR OVER SOMETHING THAT TRIVIAL, DON'T YOU SEE?

THINK OF HIS BEAUTY.
THE STRANGE-NESS OF THE SHADOW.
SUCH THINGS ARE EVERYWHERE IN THE WORLD, NOT JUST HERE AT THE MUSEUM.
DON'T YOU THINK IT WOULD BE A TERRIBLE WASTE TO PASS UP THE CHANCE...
...TO SEE SO MANY MORE OF THEM THAN THE AVERAGE PERSON?
RIGHT?
YOU WOULDN'T WANT TO *LOSE OUT* IN THAT REGARD, WOULD YOU?
GRIN
...

...I NEED TO CLEAN UP ALL THE BOTTLES.
WHEN I GET HOME...
SON OF A...
OH, WAS I THAT OBVIOUS?
YOU JUST WANT ME TO STICK AROUND AND KEEP WORKING BECAUSE THERE'S NO ONE ELSE.
YES?
WELL, FOR NOW...
TAP
YOU DO KNOW HOW TO TAKE CARE OF YOURSELF. VERY TOUGH, INDEED.
...UNTIL I'VE GOTTEN THE PAY I'VE EARNED.
I SUPPOSE I WON'T VANISH ON YOU...
END

AFTERWORD

GREETINGS TO ALL OF YOU I HAVEN'T MET BEFORE. TO THOSE FAMILIAR WITH ME, GOOD MORNIGHT.
MY NAME IS KORE YAMAZAKI.
LEMME EXPLAIN A FEW THINGS HERE...
I WANNA PLAY MINECRAFT.

THE TITLE: *FRAU FAUST.*
♂ Mann
♀ Frau
"FRAU" IS THE GERMAN WORD THAT CORRESPONDS TO "MRS."
SO IT MEANS "MRS. FAUST."

FAUST IS ONE OF THE LEGENDARY EUROPEAN ECCENTRICS.
HIS MOST FAMOUS PORTRAYAL IS IN GOETHE'S MAGNUM OPUS PLAY.
LUIS RICARDO FALERO FAUST'S DREAM (1880)

AT FIRST, I WAS GOING TO CALL IT MRS. FAUST, BUT SINCE THE WHOLE MODEL FOR THE SETTING WAS GERMANY...
I REALLY WANTED TO USE THE LANGUAGE OF THE PLACE I WAS BASING IT ON.
THEN AGAIN, I DON'T KNOW ABOUT PROPER USAGE OR HOW LANGUAGE TRENDS MIGHT HAVE CHANGED.

EDWARD JOHN POYNTER
THE VISIT OF THE QUEEN OF SHEBA TO KING SOLOMON (1890)

※COUNT OF ST. GERMAIN: A WANDERING NOBLE OF SORTS WHO APPEARS IN DIFFERENT PERIODS IN DIFFERENT FORMS.
LIKE HIS DEMON, HE IS A VERY FASCINATING CHARACTER WHO IS RIFE WITH DRAMATIC POSSIBILITIES.
COFF COFF!
IN FACT, THERE ARE A NUMBER OF GLARING SIMILARITIES TO THE COUNT OF ST. GERMAIN...
GOETHE USED THIS STORY, AND A BUNCH OF OTHERS, AS INSPIRATION FOR HIS PLAY.
FREDERIC LEIGHTON, ELIJAH IN THE WILDERNESS (1877-1878)
HE WASN'T SOME PRE-CHRISTIAN GOD, NOR WAS HE AN ANGEL.
UNLIKE THE OTHER FAMOUS DEMONS, HIS NAME DOES NOT APPEAR IN THE BIBLE.
HE IS FAUST'S DEMON, AND BELONGS ONLY TO HIM.
AS FOR MEPHISTOPHELES, I BELIEVE HIM TO BE ONE OF THE MOST WELL-KNOWN OF THE DEMONS, IF NOT THE MOST WELL-KNOWN.
MY TAKE
HAVING SAID THAT, I LOVE THE DAYTIME SOAP, SEX-AND-DEATH STYLE OF JAPANESE MYTHOLOGY, TOO!
I RECOMMEND READING THE NORSE MYTHS, AS THEY'RE QUITE FASCINATING, REALLY.
SHREWD, CALCULATING, AND YET FOOLISH AT TIMES.
PERSONALLY, I FIND HIM TO BE SIMILAR TO LOKI, THE SCANDINAVIAN TRICKSTER GOD.

EX.
- RITUAL ON NTH DAY OF X MONTH
- MUST BE ON A TUESDAY (DEPENDING ON DEMON)
- XX MUST BE SACRIFICED
- PURIFY BEFORE RITUAL
- FAST FOR X DAYS BEFORE, NO GRAINS
- LONG SPELL
- HAVE TO DRAW A MAGIC CIRCLE
- POSSESS A STRONG SPIRIT
- ETC... ETC...
...NOPE! CAN'T DO IT!
THE STEPS ARE NUMEROUS, AND RISKY.
IT'S A HIGH-DIFFICULTY UNDERTAKING FOR MOST PEOPLE. YOU HAVE TO BE ABLE TO IGNORE TEMPTATIONS.
HOWEVER, TO SUMMON A DEMON, YOU NEED CAREFUL PLANNING, A HEALTHY LIFESTYLE, AND THE KNOWLEDGE TO AVOID BEING TAKEN ADVANTAGE OF.

...AND DO NOT UNDERTAKE THIS LIGHTLY, AS IF IT'S A GAME!
IF YOU'RE CERTAIN YOU'RE GOING TO DO IT, FOLLOW ALL THE STEPS PROPERLY...
DIVINATION GAMES LIKE KOKKURI-SAN AND OUIJA BOARDS ARE DANGEROUS TOO—PARTICULARLY BECAUSE YOU DON'T TAKE THEM AS SERIOUSLY AS YOU SHOULD.
NO
BUT IT'S NOT POSSIBLE! IT'S JUST A HUGE PAIN IN THE ASS!!
I THINK IT'S IN THE NATURE OF A PERSON INTERESTED IN THE OCCULT TO WANT TO TRY OUT THE STUFF YOU'RE READING ABOUT...

CHOMP
I HOPE TO SEE YOU AGAIN IN VOLUME 2.
WELL, THANK YOU ALL FOR READING TO THE END OF THE BOOK.

NEXT ISSUE
It is the beginning of everything...
Johanna has suddenly lost consciousness.
While down, her memories flood back.
The meeting with the demon Mephistopheles.
What will Marion do when he learns the truth...?
Will the secrets of Johanna's immortality be revealed?!
MMF

JOHAN
All that remains is the head, left arm, and right leg— the journey to put Mephisto back together continues.
The inquisitors continue to harass Johanna on her travels.
What is the truth they have discovered?!
On sale November 14th, 2017
Frau Faust
2

GO ON WITH YOUR BAD SELF, JOHANNA!
~A CERTAIN UNIVERSITY'S BLACK SHEEP~
I WONDER IF FOXES REALLY DO LIKE MOUSE TEMPURA.
THOSE ARE THE MICE WE USE FOR THE LAB EXPERIMENT!!!
DON'T DO THAT!!

GO ON WITH YOUR BAD SELF, JOHANNA!
~A CERTAIN UNIVERSITY'S BLACK SHEEP~
THERE SHE GOES, WORKING ALL NIGHT AGAIN...
WHERE DID THE CATS COME FROM?

Kore Yamazaki

This is Volume 1 of *Frau Faust*. Johanna's been bouncing around in my head ever since I was a student, and now that vague idea finally has a solid form. I hope that you enjoy it.

TRANSLATION NOTES

Kuchen, page 12
The German word for "cake" or "pastry." It is pronounced koo-hen.

Geh weg!, page 44
The German phrase for "go away" or "get lost," in case the hand-shooing motion didn't make it clear already.

Kokkuri-san, page 165
Kokkuri-san is a divination game that is very similar to the Western Ouija board. The differences include using a 10-yen coin instead of a spade-shaped finder, using hiragana instead of alphabet letters, and the inclusion of a Japanese style gate (*torii*) in between the YES and NO sections of the board. Outside of those differences, the game is fairly similar in that all participants touch the main game piece, ask questions, and let forces from beyond guide the game piece in response. For quick comprehension, the example image shown in this volume was changed to the English equivalent, but the Japanese version can be seen in the image on this page.

KC KODANSHA COMICS

The Black Museum The Ghost and the Lady

By Kazuhiro Fujita

Deep in Scotland Yard in London sits an evidence room dedicated to the greatest mysteries of British history. In this "Black Museum" sits a misshapen hunk of lead—two bullets fused together—the key to a wartime encounter between Florence Nightingale, the mother of modern nursing, and a supernatural Man in Grey. This story is unknown to most scholars of history, but a special guest of the museum will tell the tale of The Ghost and the Lady...

Praise for Kazuhiro Fujita's *Ushio and Tora*

"A charming revival that combines a classic look with modern depth and pacing... **Essential viewing both for curmudgeons and new fans alike.**" — Anime News Network

"**GREAT!** The first episode of Ushio and Tora captures the essence of '90s anime." — IGN

© Kazuhiro Fujita/Kodansha Ltd. All rights reserved.

HAPPINESS

ハピネス

By **Shuzo Oshimi**

From the creator of *The Flowers of Evil*

Nothing interesting is happening in Makoto Ozaki's first year of high school. His life is a series of quiet humiliations: low-grade bullies, unreliable friends, and the constant frustration of his adolescent lust. But one night, a pale, thin girl knocks him to the ground in an alley and offers him a choice. Now everything is different. Daylight is searingly bright. Food tastes awful. And worse than anything is the terrible, consuming thirst...

Praise for Shuzo Oshimi's *The Flowers of Evil*

"A shockingly readable story that vividly—one might even say queasily—evokes the fear and confusion of discovering one's own sexuality. Recommended." —The Manga Critic

"A page-turning tale of sordid middle school blackmail." —Otaku USA Magazine

"A stunning new horror manga." —Third Eye Comics

KC KODANSHA COMICS

© Shuzo Oshimi/Kodansha Ltd. All rights reserved.

KC KODANSHA COMICS

Japan's most powerful spirit medium delves into the ghost world's greatest mysteries!

Story by Kyo Shirodaira, famed author of mystery fiction and creator of *Spiral*, *Blast of Tempest*, and *The Record of a Fallen Vampire*.

WITHDRAWN
YA-GN
FRAU FAUSTIN
462-3073

Both touched by spirits called yôkai, Kotoko and Kurô have gained unique superhuman powers. But to gain her powers Kotoko has given up an eye and a leg, and Kurô's personal life is in shambles. So when Kotoko suggests they team up to deal with renegades from the spirit world, Kurô doesn't have many other choices, but Kotoko might just have a few ulterior motives...

IN/SPECTRE

STORY BY KYO SHIRODAIRA
ART BY CHASHIBA KATASE

© Kyo Shirodaira/Kodansha Ltd. All rights reserved.

By Tomo Takeuchi

Feckless high school student Tatara Fujita wants to be good a something—anything. Unfortunately, he's about as average as a slouch teen can be. The local bullies know this, and make it a habit to hit him u for cash, but all that changes when the debonair Kaname Sengoku send them packing. Sengoku's not the neighborhood watch, though. He's professional ballroom dancer. And once Tatara Fujita gets pulled into the world of ballroom, his life will never be the same.

© Tomo Takeuchi/Kodansha Ltd. All rights reserved.

KC KODANSHA COMICS

FRANKLIN PARK PUBLIC LIBRARY
3 1316 00462 3073

Frau Faust 1 is a work of fiction. Names, characters, places, and incidents are the products of the author's imagination or are used fictitiously. Any resemblance to actual events, locales, or persons, living or dead, is entirely coincidental.

A Kodansha Comics Trade Paperback Original.

Frau Faust volume 1 copyright © 2015 Kore Yamazaki
English translation copyright © 2017 Kore Yamazaki

All rights reserved.

Published in the United States by Kodansha Comics,
an imprint of Kodansha USA Publishing, LLC, New York.

Publication rights for this English edition arranged through Kodansha Ltd., Tokyo.

First published in Japan in 2015 by Kodansha Ltd., Tokyo, as *Frau Faust* volume 1.

ISBN 978-1-63236-480-7

Printed in the United States of America.

www.kodanshacomics.com

9 8 7 6 5 4 3 2 1

Translation: Stephen Paul
Lettering: Lys Blakeslee
Editing: Ajani Oloye
Kodansha Comics edition cover design: Phil Balsman

WITHDRAWN
FRANKLIN PARK
PUBLIC LIBRARY DISTRICT
10311 GRAND AVENUE
FRANKLIN PARK, IL 60131